JOY SKIPPER

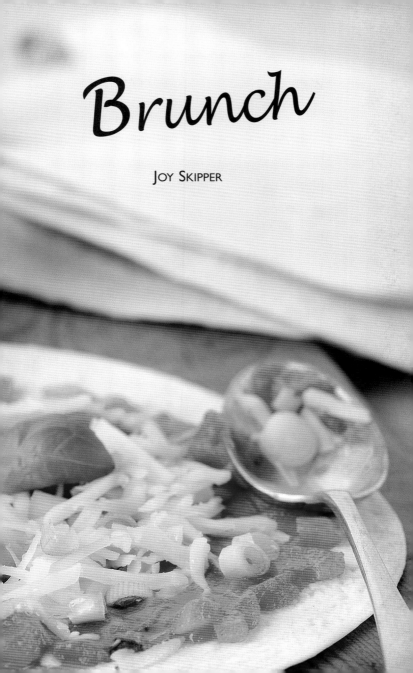

Brunch

JOY SKIPPER

First published in 2007 by
New Holland Publishers (UK) Ltd
London • Cape Town • Sydney • Auckland

Garfield House
86–88 Edgware Road
London W2 2EA
www.newhollandpublishers.com

Unit 1, 66 Gibbes Street
Chatswood
NSW 2067
Australia

80 McKenzie Street
Cape Town 8001
South Africa

218 Lake Road
Northcote, Auckland
New Zealand

ISBN 978 1845377816

Senior Editor: Clare Sayer
Photographer: Ian Garlick
Designer: Ian Sandom
Food Styling: Stella Murphy
Production: Marion Storz
Editorial Direction: Rosemary Wilkinson

Reproduction by Pica Digital PTE Ltd, Singapore
Printed and bound by Tien Wah Press, Malaysia

1 3 5 7 9 10 8 6 4 2

Contents

Introduction

Brunch is a meal that is served mid-morning, usually too late for breakfast but also to early for lunch – it is a replacement for both meals, the word 'brunch' being a portmanteau of breakfast and lunch.

Surprisingly brunch originated in Britain at the turn of the nineteenth century – the term 'brunch' was originally coined by Mr Guy Beringer in Hunters Weekly in 1895 and was not used in America until around the 1930s. In America it started as a Mother's day celebration – showing Mom how special she was by serving a lavish brunch.

As families at the turn of the nineteenth century in Britain became wealthier, the mealtimes became more extended and the food more elaborate. Brunch would have been served after a morning sporting event, such as hunting, or before an afternoon one, such as a wedding, as a more relaxed celebration than lunch. It would normally be a specially planned meal, possibly when there was a house full of guests. The food would have consisted of lots of cold cuts of meats, legs of ham or even tongue, brawn, fried potatoes or bloaters.

Now brunch is often served as a buffet-style meal, starting with the usual breakfast fare of eggs, sausages, bacon, pastries etc, but then may include other foods that are normally eaten throughout the day such as fish, salads, desserts, even large roasts. There is no rule as to what can be served – anything goes!

In New York it is perfectly normal to eat brunch after lunch time on Saturdays and Sundays and is normally associated with those trying to recover from hangovers – the food would be normal breakfast fare; eggs, pancakes, bacon etc., possibly accompanied by a Bloody Mary as a 'hair of the dog'! American Thanksgiving would be another popular time for brunch – a real family gathering with lots of autumnal foods on offer.

Alcohol does feature quite a lot with brunch, as it is often a celebration. Lots of hotels and restaurants would serve a celebration

8

Valentine or Mother's Day champagne brunch. Traditionally in some parts of England a New Year's Day brunch would consist of a dozen oysters and a Bloody Mary with yet another oyster or two dropped into it – a great way to start the year!

The Chinese serve brunch in their restaurants worldwide and this would consist of steamed, fried or baked dumplings or other sweet or savoury food items. Most restaurants serve the foods from carts that are piled high with bamboo containers – the customer takes his pick from the continuous flow of food from the kitchen.

This is a book for those who may want to make a treat for their loved one on a special day, but also for anyone planning a weekend party with a houseful of guests. The eight chapters each cover a different type of food – bread, fruit, cereal, eggs, drinks, vegetarian etc., but obviously everything can be mixed and matched. Why not make a buffet-style brunch that everybody can dip in to? For ease of preparation choose a few cold dishes such as Swiss yoghurt-soaked muesli (page 46), Fruit Danish pastry (page 24), Raspberry and banana muffins (page 20) and for the savoury lovers maybe Chorizo-stuffed tortillas (page 126), Danish open sandwich (page 140) and Mushroom crostini (page 158) – these can all be prepared pretty much in advance. And while your guests are tucking in to those you could be preparing a few hot dishes – Bacon, potato and onion sauté (page 124), Mexican scrambled eggs (page 79), Boston baked beans (page 154) and Spicy sausage patties (page 134). Serve with a few Bloody Marys and after this your guests will never want to leave.

However you want to serve brunch, this book will give you lots of ideas for recipes that will suit a number of occasions, and most recipes will tell you how to use other ingredients that you may have to hand – use the recipes as ideas and experiment each time you make them – you may invent some great recipes of your own!

Useful ingredients

Brunch can be one of those meals that you make on the spur of the moment, when friends pop over or you just get out of bed late! So it's always good to have recipes to hand that use store-cupboard ingredients, assuming your store-cupboard has a few staple ingredients plus some more interesting ones too. Eggs, cheese, bread, potatoes, fruit and vegetables can all be great ingredients to start with, and with the help of a few dried fruits, nuts and maybe even herbs from the garden, you have the start of a perfect brunch!

Bread

Bread is always great for brunch as it is so versatile, and now it is possible to buy so many varieties – flat breads such as pitta and naan, Italian breads like ciabatta and focaccia, fruit-laden breads, brioche, wholegrain, sourdough… the list is endless. And the list of things you can

make with all these breads is endless too – bruschetta or just plain cheese or scrambled eggs on toast are perfect using baguettes or any of the Italian breads. Flat breads are great as pizza bases for your own homemade pizzas – choose the toppings to suit yourself. Soaked breads to make French toast or even sweet and fruity bread pudding. Malt loaf is a meal in itself, but topped with fresh fruits it becomes a more balanced healthy way to start the day. Bagels are traditionally served with smoked salmon and cream cheese, but there is no reason why you cannot choose your own toppings depending on what is in the fridge – ham, tomato

and mayonnaise, cheese with chopped spring onion, slices of apple and a dollop of pickle, or even use the sweet ones now available and top with slices of fresh figs with blue cheese and honey.

Eggs

Of course no breakfast or brunch would be the same without eggs, whether they are boiled, scrambled, poached, fried, coddled or beaten into omelettes! Eggs are a great way to get your protein in the morning and can be used to top lots of dishes – cheese or beans on toast or grilled fish are great topped with a poached egg. And now there

are so many eggs to choose from, including omega-3 rich eggs to ensure an even healthier start to the day. For a real treat try duck eggs – they are quite a bit richer.

Herbs

Growing herbs in the garden is a great way to ensure you always have some extra flavours at hand. Use them not only to flavour your dishes, but also to add extra iron – parsley and thyme are great for this. A selection of herbs roughly chopped and added to an omelette can really make the dish. Chives stirred into scrambled eggs or crème fraîche are a great accompaniment to smoked salmon and bagels. Fresh salmon or

herrings marinated in a little oil and lime or lemon juice with freshly chopped dill is great served on pumpernickel bread. Start playing around with herbs and you will be amazed how much they can change and add to the flavour of your food.

Fruit

Having fresh fruit in the house is always good for munching on between meals. Likewise, dried fruits are great for snacking. But those healthy fruits can be made into the healthiest of brunches too, or if you really want a treat they can be made into something far naughtier! Stirred into natural yoghurt and topped with granola, or simply added to soaked

muesli or porridge are simple, great ways to ensure your fruit intake for one meal. But you can make them more interesting – try roasting strawberries, plums, figs and rhubarb with a little sprinkling of sugar or honey, and taste the difference in flavour and texture.

Make a fruit compote by simmering peaches, pears, apricot and prunes in orange juice, or even making a fruit salad with the most exotic fruits you can find. Of course one of the great ways to enjoy fruits is in a smoothie – choose your favourite combinations – bananas are always good as they tend to thicken the smoothie, but if you don't like bananas try using mango instead.

Citrus fruits add great flavour and are perfect for that morning 'zing' to wake you up! Use the rind and juice in smoothies, fruit salads, or even just poured over muesli.

Chocolate

For a self-indulgent addition to brunch, a bar of good dark chocolate can be a great store-cupboard ingredient. Always try to buy good quality dark chocolate, organic if possible. Milk chocolate does not have the same rich, bitter flavour, and white chocolate is not actually chocolate at all! Grated over warm dishes good dark chocolate will add a real bitterness and richness – grate it over warm strawberries, baked

bananas, baked figs or a selection of roasted fruits.

Melted in a small bowl over a pan of simmering water, it can also be used poured over French toast, or fruit bread or even a swirl poured into hot porridge. Grate a little over granola in the last few minutes of cooking to give a chocolate granola mixture. Make dried fruits look more appetising by dipping in melted chocolate then leave to set on greaseproof paper – these will look great served on top of fruit salad or muesli, or even just eaten as a snack.

Potatoes

Being one of the staple ingredients of our diets means that most people will have potatoes in the house most of the time. Potatoes are great for making a meal a more substantial one – add chopped cooked potatoes to an omelette with a chopped cooked onion, and you have a Spanish tortilla – great served cold cut into wedges with salad or crusty bread. Potatoes cut into wedges and roasted in olive oil are perfect served with scrambled eggs or any fish dish, or top them with cheese, melt under the grill and serve with a poached egg.

Try using sweet potatoes for a change too – they cook quicker and are healthier as well as being extremely tasty. Served them mashed with spring onions and chopped peas, wrapped in a pancake and topped with grated cheese.

Vegetables

Most vegetables can be a perfect addition to the brunch table. Mushrooms are great as there are so many varieties, giving lots of different flavours and textures. Just plain mushroom on toast does not sound wildly exciting, but fry them in garlic butter first with a sprinkling of freshly chopped herbs, then make sure the toast is thick crunchy granary or wholemeal bread, and you have a brunch that is fit for a king! When wild mushrooms are in season use a variety of them to make a creamy comforting risotto, topped with grated cheese.

Try to always use vegetables and fruits that are in season, and local if possible – this way they will have the maximum flavour as they will have had time to ripen whilst still growing, instead of in the back of a refrigerated truck! Exotic fruits tend to be higher in sugar too, as being in the sun brings out their natural sugars, so if you are trying to be healthy stick to fruits that grow closer to home.

Oats

Oats are a great ingredient for so many things, not only for brunch recipes. A great bowl of comforting porridge can be spruced up by adding fruits and honey, or chopped nuts, spices and a swirl of melted chocolate, or just quite plain with milk and sprinkled with brown sugar. Not only is it comforting, it is also good for you, with slow-releasing sugars that will give you energy throughout the day. Make it with milk, soya milk or even just water.

Making your own muesli is great as it means you know exactly what has gone into it. Oats are a good base to which you can add your favourite ingredients such as dried fruits, chopped nuts, sunflower, pumpkin or sesame seeds or shredded coconut. Play around with the ingredients and quantities until you reach a mixture that you like. And you will know each time you are eating it that there are no added extras like sugar or flavourings.

Another great use for oats is tasty flapjacks. There must be so many recipes all over the world for these –everybody has a favourite one and probably another one from their grandmothers too! Again, they can be as healthy as you want, or not. Add dried fruits, chopped nuts, seeds, chocolate chips or even chopped fresh fruits. Make them with golden syrup, honey, maple syrup or even a little treacle – the list of combinations goes on. As always it's good to experiment to find your favourite recipe.

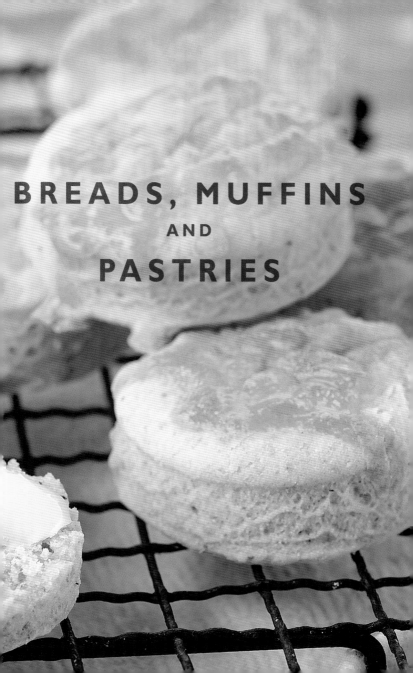

BREADS, MUFFINS
AND
PASTRIES

Raspberry and banana muffins

Most fruits work well in muffins, so you could try others too – blueberries, strawberries, blackberries and mango are all delicious cooked this way. Serve these warm with a large dollop of crème fraîche.

Makes 12

- 225 g (8 oz) plain flour
- 100 g (3½ oz) caster sugar
- 2 tsp baking powder
- Pinch of salt
- 1 egg
- 250 ml (9 fl oz) milk
- 125 ml (4½ fl oz) sunflower oil
- 1 banana, peeled and roughly chopped
- 100 g (3½ oz) fresh raspberries

1 Preheat the oven to 200°C (400°F/Gas Mark 6). Grease a muffin tin or place 12 paper cases in a muffin tin.

2 Mix together the flour, sugar, baking powder and salt in a large bowl.

3 In a separate bowl or jug beat together the egg, milk and oil.

4 Pour the wet ingredients into the dry ones and stir just until they are mixed together – do not over-mix, the mixture should still be lumpy.

5 Gently stir in the banana and raspberries.

6 Spoon the mixture into the muffin tin or paper cases and bake for 20 minutes until well risen and springy to the touch. Remove from the tin and cool on a cooling rack.

Banana and orange bread

This loaf is great served on its own but is even better spread with butter and lemon curd.

Serves 6–8

- 75 g (2¾ oz) butter
- 110 g (4 oz) caster sugar
- 1 large egg, beaten
- 225 g (8 oz) plain flour
- 2 tsp baking powder
- 4 medium bananas, peeled
- Grated rind of 2 oranges
- 50 g (1¾ oz) walnuts, chopped

1 Preheat the oven to 180°C (350°F/Gas Mark 4). Grease and base line an 8.5 cm × 19 cm (3½ in × 7½ in) loaf tin.

2 In a large bowl, cream together the butter and sugar until light and fluffy.

3 Gradually beat in the egg, making sure the mixture doesn't curdle. Sift in the flour and baking powder and gently fold them in.

4 Place the bananas in a bowl and mash to a pulp with a fork. Add to the cake mixture with the orange rind and walnuts and mix well.

5 Spoon into the prepared tin and bake for 45–55 minutes until the loaf is golden and well-risen.

6 Leave to cool in the tin for 10 minutes then turn out to cool completely on a cooling rack.

Fruit Danish

Try this pastry with strawberries and raspberries in the summer for a real treat. A sprinkling of grated nutmeg also adds a little zing!

Makes 8

- 250 g (9 oz) puff pastry
- 8 tsp apricot jam
- 2 tbsp raisins
- 2 nectarines or peaches, stoned and sliced into 8 pieces each
- 2 tsp granulated sugar

1 Preheat the oven to 200°C (400°F/Gas Mark 6).

2 Roll out the pastry to approximately 24 × 30 cm (9½ × 12 in). Cut into eight rectangles. Place the pastry rectangles onto a baking sheet.

3 Spread each piece of pastry with a tsp of apricot jam, leaving 1 cm (½ in) clear around the edge. Sprinkle over the raisins.

4 Top each one with four slices of nectarine or peach then sprinkle with sugar.

5 Bake for 20–25 minutes until golden and risen around the edge.

6 These can be eaten warm or cool on a rack to eat later.

Chocolate and banana croissants

A really naughty way to start the day – bananas and oozing chocolate in a crisp croissant – pure heaven! Dark chocolate is used here but milk or white chocolate work just as well – always buy good-quality chocolate with a high cocoa content.

Serves 4

- 4 butter croissants
- 2 bananas
- 60 g (2½ oz) good dark chocolate, roughly chopped

1 Preheat the oven to 200°C (400°F/Gas Mark 6).

2 Slice the croissants in half horizontally. Slice the bananas and divide the slices between the 4 croissants, covering the bottom half of each one. Sprinkle over the chopped chocolate, spreading it evenly. Replace the top of each croissant.

3 Place the croissants on a baking tray and bake for 8–10 minutes, until the croissant is crisp and the chocolate has melted. Serve immediately.

Challah French toast with berries

Challah is often referred to as 'egg bread' because it has lots of eggs in the recipe.

Serves 4

- 3 eggs
- 200 ml (7 fl oz) milk
- 1 tsp sugar
- 8 slices challah bread
- 125 g (4½ oz) strawberries
- 125 g (4½ oz) blueberries
- 125 g (4½ oz) raspberries
- 100 g (3½ oz) blackberries
- 2 tsp caster sugar
- Juice and grated rind of 1 lemon
- 75 g (2¾ oz) unsalted butter
- Dusting of icing sugar to serve

1 Whisk together the eggs, milk and sugar in a large shallow dish.

2 Add the bread slices to the bowl. Leave to soak for about 6 minutes, turning each slice once.

3 Meanwhile place half the fruit in a food processor with the sugar and lemon juice and rind and blitz briefly to break up the fruits. Transfer to a bowl and stir in the whole fruits. Leave to one side.

4 Melt a quarter of the butter in a frying pan and when it is foaming add the slices of bread (however many will fit into the pan). Cook for about 1 minute on either side, or until golden brown. Keep those slices warm while you melt more butter and repeat with the other slices until all the slices are cooked.

5 Serve the warm French toast with the summer fruits spooned over the top – dust with icing sugar if required.

Ham and cheese croissants

A great way to turn croissants into a more substantial meal – you can also add tomatoes, or other meats or a variety of cheeses – but make sure the cheese is of the melting kind.

Serves 4

- 4 butter croissants
- 4 slices ham
  (8 if very thin slices)
- 2 tsp mustard
- 125 g (4½ oz) cheddar
  cheese, grated

1 Preheat the oven to 200°C (400°F/Gas Mark 6).

2 Slice the croissants in half horizontally. Divide the ham between the croissants and place on the bottom half of each one. Spread with the mustard and then top with the grated cheese.

3 Replace the tops of each croissant and place each one on a baking tray. Bake for 6–8 minutes until the croissant is crisp and the cheese is melting. Serve hot.

Cheese and herb scones

These are best made with a really strong cheddar cheese, but you could also substitute blue cheese if you prefer.

Makes 12

- 50 g (1¾ oz) butter
- 225 g (8 oz) plain white flour
- Pinch of salt
- 1 tsp baking powder
- 110 g (4 oz) strong cheddar cheese
- 1 tsp English mustard powder
- 2 tsp fresh thyme leaves
- Pinch of cayenne
- 125–150 ml (4–5 fl oz) milk

1 Preheat the oven to 200°C (400°F/Gas Mark 6).

2 Place the butter, flour, salt and baking powder into a food processor and blitz until the butter is worked into the flour and the mixture resembles breadcrumbs.

3 Add two-thirds of the cheese, mustard powder, thyme and cayenne and 'pulse' once or twice to mix them in.

4 With the machine running, add the milk gradually until the dough comes together – do not overwork it.

5 Tip out onto a floured work surface and roll or press out to a thickness of 1.5 cm (¾ in). Cut into rounds with a pastry cutter or glass approximately 8 cm (3 in) in diameter and place on a baking sheet.

6 Sprinkle with the remaining cheese and bake for 12–15 minutes until golden. Eat while still warm with butter.

Cheese and tomato toastie

A very indulgent melting cheese sandwich that is really delicious. Most cheeses work well cooked this way so experiment with your favourites.

Serves 1

- 2 large slices white bread, buttered
- 2 tbsp tomato relish
- 50 g (1¾ oz) Gruyère cheese, grated
- 1 tomato, thinly sliced
- 15 g (½ oz) butter, melted
- 25 g (1 oz) Parmesan, grated

1 Preheat the grill to the highest setting.

2 Spread both slices of bread with the tomato relish then sprinkle one slice with grated Gruyère cheese. Add a layer of sliced tomato and place the other slice of bread on top.

3 Brush the top of the sandwich with half the melted butter then sprinkle with half the Parmesan, pressing it down lightly to help it stick.

4 Grill for 1–2 minutes until golden then turn the sandwich over and repeat with the remaining butter and Parmesan. Eat while still hot.

Roasted pepper and goats cheese bruschetta

Roast peppers are very easy and really delicious, but if you want a really quick snack you can also buy them in jars already roasted. These could also be served as a light snack or pre-dinner nibble.

Serves 4

- 2 red peppers, deseeded and halved
- 1 yellow pepper, deseeded and halved
- 8 slices ciabatta or French baguette
- 2 cloves garlic, peeled and halved
- 100 g (3½ oz) goats cheese, crumbled
- 4 tbsp olive oil
- Basil leaves to serve

1 Place the halves of pepper under a hot grill and cook until blackened. Place in a bowl and cover with cling film and leave to cool.

2 When the peppers are cool enough to handle, peel off the blackened skin and slice the flesh.

3 Toast the bread until crisp on both sides and then rub with the garlic cloves.

4 Divide the roast pepper strips between the bruschetta and crumble over the cheese.

5 Drizzle with olive oil and place under the grill for 2–3 minutes.

6 Serve scattered with torn basil leaves.

Brunch quesadillas

Quesadillas can be stuffed with lots of foods, try adding chicken or prawns to this dish – always use cheese though as the melting bit is the best!

Serves 2

- 350 g (12 oz) baby spinach leaves
- 4 flour tortillas
- 125 g (4½ oz) tomato salsa
- 200 g (7 oz) cheddar cheese, grated

1 Cook the spinach in a tiny amount of water until wilted. Drain and squeeze out all the water.

2 Place two of the tortillas on the work surface and divide the spinach between them, spreading it over the whole tortilla.

3 Spoon the salsa over the spinach, again spreading over the whole tortilla.

4 Sprinkle each one with cheese and top with the remaining tortillas.

5 Heat a griddle pan and cook the quesadillas until the cheese starts to melt and the tortillas start to turn brown. Turn over and cook the other side until golden brown.

6 Turn out onto a chopping board and cut into wedges.

Toasted panettone with hot prunes

Panettone is a light sweet Italian bread containing candied fruits and sultanas. For anybody with a sweet tooth, this is a must! The prunes are also great served cold with natural yoghurt.

Serves 4

- 300 g (10½ oz) pitted prunes
- 1 orange
- 2 tsp honey
- 4 slices Panettone
- Crème fraîche to serve
- Grated nutmeg to serve

1 Place the prunes in a small pan. Cut the rind off the orange using a vegetable peeler to ensure no white pith. Cut the peel into julienne strips and add to the pan.

2 Juice the remaining orange and pour the juice over the prunes. Add the honey, bring to the boil and then simmer for 12–15 minutes.

3 Toast the Panettone, place on 4 plates and spoon over the hot prunes.

4 Serve with a dollop of crème fraîche sprinkled with a pinch of grated nutmeg.

Parma ham bruschetta

Bruschetta is great for serving lots of things – vary your toppings from fish, meat, roasted vegetables, cheese and salads. The name reflects its original cooking method derived from the Italian word for 'roast over coals'.

Makes 8

- 8 slices ciabatta or French baguette
- 2 cloves garlic, peeled and halved
- 4 tomatoes, halved
- 8 slices Parma ham
- 4 tbsp olive oil
- Freshly ground black pepper

1 Toast the slices of bread until crisp on both sides.

2 Rub each slice firstly with the cloves of garlic and then with the tomato, using a fork to mash the tomato into the bread.

3 Top each slice with a slice of Parma ham, drizzle with olive oil and serve sprinkled with freshly ground black pepper.

Chocolate brownies

In Australia and New Zealand a brownie is fruit currant bread. But all Americans know a true brownie is full of gooey chocolate! A real treat to eat for brunch – nobody will be able to resist these.

Makes about 16

300 g (10¹/₂ oz) caster sugar
4 eggs
225 g (8 oz) unsalted butter, melted
75 g (2³/₄ oz) cocoa powder
75 g (2³/₄ oz) plain flour
225 g (8 oz) plain chocolate
100 g (3¹/₂ oz) pecans, chopped

1 Preheat the oven to 180°C (350°F/Gas Mark 4). Grease a 20-cm (8-in) tin.

2 Beat together the sugar and eggs until the sugar has completely dissolved.

3 Whisk the butter into the egg mixture.

4 Sieve together the cocoa and flour and stir into the egg mixture.

5 Melt the chocolate in a bowl over a pan of simmering water then stir it into the egg mixture, along with the chopped pecans.

6 Pour into the greased tin and bake for 25–35 minutes until a knife pierced in the centre comes out nearly clean (you want the centre to be a little bit gooey).

7 Leave to cool in the tin before removing and cutting into squares or slices.

CEREALS

Honey granola

Granola is like a crisp, sweeter version of muesli and can contain different dried fruits and nuts. This one is great served layered in a glass or bowl, with fruit compote and yoghurt. Having oats for brunch is also a good way of keeping your energy level up for the day.

Serves 6–8

- 1½ tbsp honey
- 1½ tbsp maple syrup
- 1 tbsp sunflower oil
- 1 tbsp warm water
- 3 tbsp dark muscovado sugar
- Pinch of salt
- 110 g (4 oz) jumbo oats
- 55 g (2 oz) whole almonds
- 30 g (1¼ oz) whole brazil nuts, chopped

1 Preheat the oven to 140°C (275°F/Gas Mark 1).

2 Whisk together the honey, maple syrup, oil, water, sugar and salt in a large bowl.

3 Stir in the remaining ingredients and mix really well.

4 Spread the mixture on a baking tray lined with greaseproof paper and bake for 20–30 minutes, stirring after 15 minutes. Keep an eye on the cooking time as the mixture can burn quite easily.

5 Leave to cool on the baking tray before storing in an airtight container.

6 Serve with fruits and yoghurt.

Swiss yoghurty muesli

This is such a healthy brunch or breakfast dish – it has lots of great nutrients and will keep your energy levels up for hours as soaking the fruits and nuts in yoghurt helps the enzymes to start their work before it reaches your body!

Serves 4–6

- 50 g (2 oz) wheat flakes
- 25 g (1 oz) toasted bran
- 25 g (1 oz) medium porridge oats
- 25 g (1 oz) dried cranberries
- 25 g (1 oz) raisins
- 25 g (1 oz) walnuts, chopped
- 50 g (2 oz) dried apricots, diced
- 2 apples peeled and grated
- 200 ml (7 fl oz) natural yoghurt
- 300 ml (½ pt) milk
- Fresh fruits to serve

1 Mix together all the dry ingredients in a large bowl.

2 Stir in the grated apple, yoghurt and milk. Leave to stand for 20 minutes or overnight if possible – the soaking makes the muesli more easily digestible and therefore even healthier.

3 Serve with chopped fresh fruits of your choice.

Seed-filled flapjacks

Filled with sunflower and pumpkin seeds these flapjacks are full of omega-3 oils that will keep you healthy. Perfect for a brunch on the move or picnic brunch.

Makes 16

- 100 ml (3½ fl oz) sunflower oil
- 30 g (1¼ oz) light soft brown sugar
- 150 g (5½ oz) golden syrup
- 250 g (9 oz) oats
- 50 g (2 oz) pumpkin seeds
- 50 g (2 oz) sunflower seeds
- 50 g (2 oz) dried fruits (raisins, cranberries, chopped apricots)

1 Preheat the oven to 180°C (350°F/Gas Mark 4). Grease a 20-cm (8-in) square tin.

2 Put the oil, sugar and syrup into a pan and heat very gently to dissolve the sugar.

3 Add the remaining ingredients and mix well.

4 Pour into the prepared tin and cook for 15–18 minutes until set and golden.

5 Leave to cool for 10 minutes before marking into squares then leave to cool completely.

6 Turn out of the tin, break into squares and store in an airtight container.

Cinnamon and pecan porridge

A traditional Scottish dish that everybody has their own version of! This warming winter breakfast or brunch is really creamy topped with spicy nuts to give that extra 'bite'.

Serves 2

- 200 g (7 oz) porridge oats
- 600 ml (1 pt) milk
- 300 ml (½ pt) water
- 50 g (2 oz) pecan nuts
- ¼ tsp ground cinnamon
- 25 g (1 oz) dark muscovado sugar

1 Put the oats, milk and water into a pan and bring up to the boil then reduce the heat and simmer gently, stirring frequently, until the mixture thickens.

2 Meanwhile toast the pecan nuts in a small frying pan with the ground cinnamon – keep an eye on them because they will burn quickly – they just need to be slightly browned.

3 Pour the porridge into two bowls. Take the pecans off the heat and stir in the muscovado sugar before sprinkling over the porridge. Serve hot.

Spiced date porridge

A great way of spicing up a bowl of porridge, with soft,
luscious dates for added flavour. For a special occasion pour
over a spoonful of double cream when serving.

Serves 2

- 200 g (7 oz) porridge oats
- 600 ml (1 pt) water
- 50 g (2 oz) Medjool
  dates, chopped
- ¼ tsp ground cinnamon
- Pinch of ground nutmeg
- 2 tbsp honey
- 2 tbsp cream

1 Put the oats and water into a saucepan
and bring to the boil then reduce the
heat and simmer for about 5 minutes,
stirring frequently, until the mixture
thickens.

2 Add the dates and spices and cook,
stirring, for another 2 minutes.

3 Pour into two bowls and spoon over the
honey and cream to serve.

Quinoa stuffed tomatoes

Pronounced "keen-wa", quinoa is a grain that comes from the Andes in South America, where is it known as a 'supergrain' due to its high protein content.

Serves 6

- 125 g (4¹/₂ oz) quinoa
- 300 ml (¹/₂ pt) vegetable stock
- 1 tbsp olive oil
- 1 small red onion, peeled and diced
- 50 g (2 oz) mushrooms, diced
- ¹/₂ tsp ground cumin
- 25 g (1 oz) pine nuts, toasted
- 6 beef tomatoes
- 75 g (3 oz) cheddar cheese, grated

1 Preheat the oven to 200°C (400°F/Gas Mark 6).

2 Place the quinoa and stock in a pan, bring to the boil then simmer for 15 minutes.

3 Meanwhile heat the oil in a frying pan and sauté the red onion for 2–3 minutes before adding the mushrooms and ground cumin. Cook for another 2–3 minutes before stirring in the pine nuts.

4 Drain the quinoa, return to the pan and then stir in the mushroom mixture.

5 Cut the tops off the tomatoes and scoop out the fleshy centres – chop the flesh and add to the quinoa along with the grated cheese, mix well.

6 Spoon the quinoa into the tomatoes, pressing down. Balance the tops back on to the tomatoes to keep the moisture in and bake for 20–25 minutes.

Cheese-stuffed mushrooms

These are great cooked in the oven but even better on a summer brunch barbecue.

Serves 4

- 125 g (4½ oz) couscous
- 4 large Portobello mushrooms
- 1 tbsp olive oil
- 1 onion, peeled and chopped
- 2 tomatoes, chopped
- 125 g (4½ oz) goats cheese, crumbled
- 1 tbsp freshly chopped parsley or chives
- Salt and freshly ground black pepper

1 Preheat the oven to 200°C (400°F/Gas Mark 6).

2 Place the couscous in a bowl and cover with boiling water. Leave to stand for 10–15 minutes. Cut the stalks from the mushrooms and chop.

3 Heat the oil in a frying pan and sauté the onion for 5–6 minutes, until soft. Add the tomato and chopped mushroom stalks and cook for 1–2 minutes.

4 Fluff up the couscous with a fork and add the sautéed onion and tomato. Mix in the crumbled goats cheese and freshly chopped parsley or chives. Check the seasoning.

5 Divide the couscous mixture between the 4 mushrooms, patting it down well.

6 Bake for 10–15 minutes until the mushroom is cooked and the topping is melting and golden.

Dried fruit compote with granola

Dried fruits are great for cooking this way, they become syrupy and very sweet – you can also stir in some fresh fruit when the compote is chilled, if you need to make it go further.

Serves 4

- 110 g (4 oz) prunes, stones removed
- 110 g (4 oz) dried apricots
- 110 g (4 oz) dried figs
- 50 g (1 ³/₄ oz) raisins
- 2 rose hip tea bags
- 2 tbsp honey
- 4 cloves
- 300 g (10 oz) natural yoghurt
- Grated zest of 1 lemon
- 4 tbsp Honey granola (see page 44)

1 Place the fruit in a pan with the tea bags, honey and cloves. Pour in water to just cover the fruit. Bring to the boil and simmer for 20 minutes.

2 Remove the tea bags and leave the fruit to cool. Remove the fruit with a slotted spoon and divide between four bowls.

3 Mix together the yoghurt and lemon zest and add a dollop to each bowl of fruit.

4 Sprinkle with the honey granola and serve.

Birchermuesli

Dr Bircher advocated that healthcare was more than just medical treatment and invented this recipe for his patients – it is now one of Switzerland's most widely eaten dishes around the world. It is a really filling but very healthy brunch.

Serves 6–8

- 1 banana, peeled and sliced
- 1 apple, cored and chopped
- Juice of $\frac{1}{2}$ lemon
- 100 g (3$\frac{1}{2}$ oz) blueberries
- 100 g (3$\frac{1}{2}$ oz) raspberries
- 100 g (3$\frac{1}{2}$ oz) walnuts, roughly chopped
- 175 g (6 oz) rolled oats
- $\frac{1}{4}$ tsp ground cinnamon
- 400 g (14 oz) natural or fruit flavoured yoghurt

1 Squeeze the lemon juice over the sliced banana and apple to stop the fruits going brown. Place the fruit, nuts, oats and ground cinnamon in a bowl and mix well.

2 To serve, layer the fruit and nut mixture with yoghurt in glasses or bowls, ending with a small sprinkling of the fruit and nut mixture on top. This can be mixed together completely but looks much nicer served in layers.

EGGS

Eggs Benedict

This is a very traditional brunch or breakfast dish, said to date back to the 1960s in America. Don't be scared of making hollandaise sauce as it is really very easy.

Serves 4

Hollandaise sauce
- 2 large egg yolks
- Salt and freshly ground black pepper
- 2 tsp lemon juice
- 2 tsp white wine vinegar
- 110 g (4 oz) butter

- 4 large fresh eggs
- 8 slices pancetta
- 2 English muffins, split in half horizontally

1 To make the hollandaise sauce, place the eggs in blender with the seasoning and blend for 1 minute.

2 Heat the lemon juice and white wine vinegar to a simmer in a small pan. Pour this slowly into the blender whilst it is running.

3 Melt the butter in the same small pan and pour this into the running blender in a thin, slow trickle. This will give you a thick, smooth buttery sauce.

4 Poach the eggs in boiling water. Grill the pancetta until crisp and toast the muffin halves on both sides until golden.

5 Top each half of muffin with 2 pieces of pancetta and a poached egg.

6 Pour over the hollandaise sauce and flash under a hot grill for 30 seconds then serve immediately.

Eggs Florentine

Another very traditional brunch dish – spinach topped with a poached egg and cheesey sauce. For a summer treat, try it with some fresh crabmeat stirred into the spinach.

Serves 4

Cheese sauce

- 20 g (³/₄ oz) butter
- 20 g (³/₄ oz) flour
- Pinch of mustard powder
- 300 ml (¹/₂ pt) milk
- 75 g (3 oz) strong cheddar, grated

- 450 g (1 lb) fresh spinach, cooked and chopped
- 15 g (¹/₂ oz) butter, melted
- Salt and freshly ground black pepper
- Pinch of grated nutmeg
- 4 large eggs

1 To make the cheese sauce, melt the butter in a pan and stir in the flour and mustard powder. Cook, stirring for 1 minute to make a roux.

2 Pour in the milk and whisk to remove any lumps of flour, and then cook over a gentle heat, stirring continuously, until it begins to boil.

3 Turn the heat down to a simmer and stir in 55 g (2 oz) of the cheese – you should have a thick, smooth creamy cheese sauce.

4 Make sure the cooked spinach is well drained and then turn in the melted butter and season with salt, pepper and nutmeg. Place in an ovenproof dish.

5 Softly poach the eggs then drain and place them on top of the spinach. Pour over the cheese sauce and sprinkle with the remaining cheese.

Place under a hot grill and cook until golden and bubbling. Serve immediately, with crusty brown bread to mop up the juices.

Herb baked eggs

These are great for children – a fun way to get them to eat eggs, with a little cream and some herbs, all served up in a neat ramekin.

Serves 4

- 50 g (1³/₄ oz) butter
- 1 shallot, finely chopped
- 100 g (3¹/₂ oz) mushrooms, chopped
- 1 tsp freshly chopped parsley
- 1 tsp freshly chopped chives
- Salt and freshly ground black pepper
- 4 large eggs
- 4 tbsp single cream

1 Preheat the oven to 180°C (350°F/Gas Mark 4). Lightly butter 4 ramekin dishes.

2 Melt the remaining butter and cook the shallot for 1–2 minutes until soft.

3 Add the mushrooms and cook for another 3–4 minutes. Add the herbs and seasoning.

4 Divide the mushroom mixture between the 4 ramekin dishes, making a dip in the centre of each. Break an egg into each dish and top with a tablespoon of single cream.

5 Stand the dishes in a roasting pan half-filled with hot water and bake for 10–15 minutes until the whites are just set and the yolks still runny. Serve with crusty bread.

Brunch tortilla

Tortilla is the Spanish version of an omelette and the filling can be varied to include roast peppers, onions, ham, chicken or even prawns and fish. This can also be eaten cold so is perfect for taking on a picnic.

Serves 4–6

- 4 tbsp olive oil
- 4 rashers bacon, chopped
- 425 g (15 oz) potatoes, peeled and diced
- 6 large eggs
- 150 g (5½ oz) cherry tomatoes, halved
- Salt and freshly ground black pepper
- Chopped fresh parsley to garnish

1 Heat half the oil in a frying pan and cook the bacon for 6–8 minutes. Remove with a slotted spoon.

2 Add the potatoes to the pan, lower the heat and cook for 12–15 minutes, turning occasionally, until they are cooked through. Remove with a slotted spoon.

3 Beat the eggs in a large bowl with the seasoning and stir in the bacon, potatoes and tomato halves.

4 Heat the remaining oil in the frying pan again, and pour the egg mixture into it whilst on a high heat. Cook for 1–2 minutes before turning the temperature down.

5 Cook for 12–15 minutes, keeping an eye on the edges to make sure it is not getting too cooked underneath – the top will still be runny.

6 Place the pan under a preheated grill and cook the top until it is golden and bubbling.

7 To turn out of the pan, place a plate on top and turn upside down. Cut into wedges to serve.

Omelette Arnold Bennett

Originally served as a late supper dish at the Savoy Hotel for the famous novelist Arnold Bennett himself! Traditionally smoked haddock was used but any smoked fish would be just as delicious.

Serves 1

- 75 g (3 oz) smoked haddock
- 100 ml (3½ fl oz) milk
- 1 tbsp Parmesan, grated
- 3 eggs
- Salt and freshly ground black pepper
- 15 g (½ oz) butter
- 1 tbsp double cream
- Fresh dill to garnish

1 Poach the smoked haddock in the milk for 10 minutes, then drain and gently flake the fish into large chunks, removing any skin and bones, and mix with the grated parmesan.

2 Preheat the grill. Break the eggs into a bowl and gently whisk with 1 tbsp of water and the seasoning.

3 Melt the butter in a frying pan and when bubbling add the eggs.

4 Add the fish and cheese on top of the eggs when they begin to set.

5 Pour the cream over while the eggs are still a little liquid and place the omelette pan under the grill. Grill until golden then slide onto a hot plate and serve immediately.

Bacon and chive scrambled eggs

A twist on straight scrambled eggs – more flavour and great taste. Serve on toasted bread or with grilled tomatoes and black pudding.

Serves 2

- 4 rashers streaky bacon, chopped into bite-size pieces
- 4 large eggs
- 4 tbsp milk
- 2 tbsp freshly chopped chives
- Seasoning
- Knob of butter

1 Grill the bacon until crisp.

2 Meanwhile, beat the eggs with the milk, chives and seasoning in a bowl.

3 Melt the butter in a saucepan. Pour in the egg mixture and cook slowly over a low heat, stirring constantly. When nearly set, stir in the bacon.

4 Serve on toasted bread with grilled tomatoes.

Herb omelette

Any herbs can be used in an omelette, but always use fresh ones as the dried variety are too strong for this – pick your favourites and chop them well.

Serves 1

- 2 eggs, very lightly beaten
- Salt and freshly ground pepper
- 1 tbsp freshly chopped parsley
- 1 tbsp freshly chopped chives
- 15 g (½ oz) butter

1 Gently mix together the eggs, seasoning, parsley and chives.

2 Heat a small frying pan and add the butter – swirl it around to coat the whole pan.

3 Pour in the eggs and shake the pan to spread them out evenly then, using a fork draw the edges of the omelette to the centre, allowing uncooked egg to reach the pan.

4 When the omelette is nearly cooked and the top is slightly liquid, tilt the pan with one hand and use a palette knife to flip over one edge of the omelette into the centre.

5 Slide it out of the pan onto a plate and serve immediately.

Parmesan crusted asparagus and poached egg

This is a great way to enjoy asparagus when it is in season. This could also be served as a starter or light lunch.

Serves 4

- 450 g (1 lb) fresh asparagus, trimmed
- 4 eggs
- 75 g (2¾ oz) Parmesan, grated
- Freshly ground black pepper

1 Steam the asparagus in an asparagus steamer if you have one. If not, cook in boiling water for 5–6 minutes, until tender but not soft. Drain.

2 Poach the eggs in boiling water and keep warm.

3 Preheat the grill and line a baking sheet with foil. Place the asparagus on the foil and sprinkle with half the grated Parmesan. Grill for 3–4 minutes before turning the asparagus and sprinkling with the remaining Parmesan. Grill again for 3–4 minutes or until the cheese starts to turn golden.

4 Divide the asparagus between 4 plates and top with a poached egg on each. Sprinkle with freshly ground black pepper and serve immediately.

Creamy egg and onion bruschetta

Perfect for a buffet style brunch – these can be served with a selection of other crostini (see page 158).

Makes 12

- 1 ciabatta loaf, cut into 12 thin slices
- 6 tbsp olive oil
- 4 tbsp single cream
- 4 spring onions, sliced
- 25 g (1 oz) butter
- 4 large eggs
- Salt and freshly ground black pepper
- Chopped fresh parsley to serve

1 Toast the slices of bread on both sides then drizzle with olive oil.

2 Place the single cream in a bowl with the spring onions.

3 Melt the butter in a pan. Break the eggs into a bowl and whisk lightly with a fork.

4 When the butter is foaming pour the eggs in and stir gently but continuously until they start to solidify.

5 Pour in the cream and spring onions and continue to cook and stir until all the liquid has gone.

6 Check for seasoning then spoon the creamy egg onto the brushcetta, sprinkle with chopped parsley and serve immediately.

Mexican eggs

Great served with thick crusty bread to mop up all the
juices. If you want a little more spice in the morning
add ½ chopped red chilli with the onion.

Serves 4

5 eggs
100 g (3½ oz) butter
2 onions, peeled
and chopped
1 green pepper, deseeded
and chopped
300 g (11 oz) tinned
sweetcorn, drained
1 tbsp tomato pickle or salsa
Salt and freshly ground
black pepper
1 tbsp plain flour
250 ml (9 fl oz) milk
4 tbsp double cream
75 g (3 oz) cheddar cheese,
grated

1 Softly boil the eggs, shell them and keep
them in warm water.

2 Melt 75 g (2¾ oz) of the butter in a
frying pan and sauté the onion for 6–7
minutes until just starting to turn golden,
then add the green pepper and
sweetcorn and cook for 1–2 minutes. Stir
in the pickle or salsa and season.

3 Melt the remaining butter in a small pan
then stir in the flour to make a roux.
Whisk in the milk and continue to stir
until the sauce boils and thickens.

4 Remove from the heat and stir in half the
cheese.

5 Spoon the corn mixture into an
ovenproof dish, drain the eggs and place
on top. Cover with the sauce and sprinkle
with the remaining cheese.

6 Cook under a hot grill until brown and
bubbling. Serve hot.

Poached egg on cheesey toast

Forget thin slices of cheese on toast – this cheesey toast is creamy and punchy, topped with a softly poached egg. Delicious served with tomato ketchup!

Serves 4

- 225 g (8 oz) cheddar cheese, grated
- 2 tbsp milk
- 1 tsp Worcestershire Sauce
- 1 tsp mustard
- 1 pinch paprika
- 2 tsp freshly chopped chives
- 4 thick slices wholemeal bread
- 4 eggs

1 Preheat the grill. Bring a pan of water to the boil for the poached eggs.

2 Mix together the cheese, milk, Worcestershire sauce, mustard and paprika and half of the chives – stir until well combined.

3 Toast the slices of bread on one side. Turn the bread over and spread with the cheese mixture. Place the eggs in the boiling water to poach.

4 Return the bread topped with cheese to the grill and cook until the cheese is bubbling and golden.

5 Place each of the cheesey toast on a plate and top each one with a poached egg.

6 Sprinkle with the remaining chives and serve.

PANCAKES
AND
WAFFLES

Blueberry pancakes with maple syrup

Blueberries are one of the best anti-oxidants you can eat – so although this recipe feels a little naughty, you can imagine that a small part of it is doing you some good.

Serves 4–6

- 125 g (4½ oz) self-raising flour
- 3 tbsp caster sugar
- 1 tsp bicarbonate of soda
- 1 egg
- 40 g (1½ oz) butter, melted
- 350 ml (12 fl oz) buttermilk
- Grated rind of 1 lemon
- 250 g (9 oz) blueberries
- Vegetable oil for frying
- Maple syrup to serve

1 Place the flour, sugar and bicarbonate of soda in a bowl and mix together.

2 Whisk together the egg, butter and buttermilk in a separate bowl.

3 Pour the wet ingredients into the dry and mix well until smooth.

4 Gently stir the lemon rind and the blueberries into the batter, keeping a few blueberries aside to serve.

5 Heat a frying pan and wipe with a little oil. Pour spoonfuls of the batter into the pan and cook for 1–2 minutes on each side, using a palette knife to turn them over, until golden. Cook in batches, keeping them warm until you have used all the batter.

6 Serve the pancakes drizzled with maple syrup

Fruit stuffed pancakes

Pancakes are so versatile and can be stuffed with so many things, savoury or sweet. If you can't get hold of fresh raspberries, use defrosted frozen fruits.

Makes 8

- 100 g (3½ oz) plain flour
- 2 medium eggs
- 200 ml (7 fl oz) milk
- 75 ml (2½ fl oz) water
- 1 tsp vegetable oil for frying pancakes
- Grated rind of 1 orange
- 250 g (9 oz) low fat natural yoghurt
- 500 g (1 lb 2 oz) fresh raspberries
- 1 tsp muscovado sugar
- Pinch of cinnamon

1 Put the flour in a bowl and make a well in the centre. Break the eggs into the well and start to whisk, bringing in the flour from the edges.

2 Mix the milk and water together in a jug and gradually pour this mixture into the bowl, whisking continuously until you have a smooth batter. Leave to stand for 10 minutes.

3 Heat a non-stick frying pan (or crêpe pan) and pour in a tiny amount of vegetable oil. Wipe with kitchen paper to take away any excess.

4 Pour a ladle of the batter into the hot pan and swirl around until the whole base of the pan is coated. Cook for 4–5 minutes then flip over with a palette knife (or toss!) and cook for 2–3 minutes. Keep each pancake warm wrapped in greaseproof paper while you repeat with the remaining batter.

5 Stir the grated orange rind into the natural yoghurt.

6 Spoon 1–2 tbsp of the raspberries on to each pancake and fold into quarters.

7 Spoon a dollop of orange flavoured yoghurt on to each one and sprinkle with a little muscovado sugar mixed with cinnamon to serve.

Pancakes with cheese and mushroom

The pancakes can be made in advance and heated in the oven or microwave when needed. Use a good strong Cheddar that melts and oozes out of the pancakes.

Makes 8

- 1 tbsp olive oil
- 15 g (1/2 oz) butter
- 200 g (7 oz) chestnut mushrooms, sliced
- 100 g (3 1/2 oz) plain flour
- 2 medium eggs
- 200 ml (7 fl oz) milk
- 75 ml (2 1/2 fl oz) water
- 1 tsp vegetable oil for frying pancakes
- 175 g (6 oz) cheddar cheese, grated

1 Heat the olive oil and butter in a frying pan and cook the mushrooms for 6–8 minutes, until slightly browning. Remove from the pan and set aside.

2 Put the flour in a bowl and make a well in the centre. Break the eggs into the well and start to whisk, bringing in the flour from the edges.

3 Mix the milk and water together in a jug and gradually pour this mixture into the bowl, whisking continuously until you have a smooth batter. Leave to stand for 10 minutes.

4 Heat a non-stick frying pan (or crêpe pan) and pour in a tiny amount of vegetable oil. Wipe with kitchen paper to take away any excess.

Pour a ladle of the batter into the hot pan and swirl around until the whole base of the pan is coated. Cook for 4–5 minutes then flip over with a palette knife or toss.

6 Cover just over a quarter of the pancake with cooked mushrooms and sprinkle with cheese. Cook for 2–3 minutes. Fold the pancake into quarters whilst still in the pan. Serve warm.

Banana and chocolate pancakes

This is really self-indulgent – fresh pancakes oozing with melted chocolate and softening banana.

Makes 8

- 100 g (3½ oz) plain flour
- 2 medium eggs
- 200 ml (7 fl oz) milk
- 75 ml (2½ fl oz) water
- 1 tsp muscovado sugar
- Pinch of cinnamon
- 1 tsp vegetable oil for frying pancakes
- 4 bananas, chopped
- 150 g (5½ oz) dark chocolate, chopped
- Icing sugar to serve

1 Put the flour in a bowl and make a well in the centre. Break the eggs into the well and start to whisk, bringing in the flour from the edges.

2 Mix the milk and water together in a jug and gradually pour this mixture into the bowl, whisking continuously until you have a smooth batter.

3 Heat a non-stick frying pan (or crêpe pan) and pour in a tiny amount of vegetable oil. Wipe with kitchen paper to take away any excess.

4 Pour a ladle of the batter into the hot pan and swirl around until the base of the pan is coated. Cook for 4–5 minutes then flip over with a palette knife.

5 Cover half of the pancake with chopped banana and sprinkle with chopped chocolate. Cook for 2–3 minutes. Fold the pancake over whilst still in the pan. Serve warm sprinkled with icing sugar.

Peaches and cream topped waffles

This is perfect for those with a sweet tooth – the addition of a little alcohol also makes it great for a special occasion. If you have time, any of the waffle recipes in the book can be used (see pages 94 and 96), or if you are in a hurry use shop bought ones.

Serves 4

- 8 ripe peaches, stoned and cut into quarters
- 4 tbsp honey
- 1/2 tsp ground cinnamon
- 200 ml (7 fl oz) double cream
- 1 tbsp Kahlua or Tia Maria
- 8 waffles (homemade or shop bought)
- Toasted almond slivers to serve

1 Preheat the oven to 200°C (400°F/Gas Mark 6).

2 Place the peach quarters in a roasting tin, drizzle with the honey and sprinkle with ground cinnamon. Place in the oven and roast for 20–25 minutes until starting to caramelize.

3 Whisk the cream and liqueur together until soft peaks form.

4 Toast the waffles, top with the roast peaches and a dollop of tipsy cream. Sprinkle with toasted almond slivers and serve immediately.

Orange and pecan waffles

Pecans are the nuts of the hickory tree, grown mainly in Mexico and southern USA. Here they are cooked in waffle batter and topped with orange segments.

Makes 20

- 600 g (1 lb 5 oz) plain flour
- 50 g (1 3/4 oz) granulated sugar
- 4 tsp baking powder
- 2 tsp bicarbonate of soda
- 1 tsp salt
- 4 eggs, lightly beaten
- 175 ml (6 fl oz) vegetable oil
- 450 g (1 lb) low-fat natural yoghurt
- 350 ml (12 fl oz) milk
- 100 g (3 1/2 oz) chopped pecans
- 4 oranges
- Natural yoghurt to serve
- Caster sugar for sprinkling

1 Combine the flour, sugar, baking powder, bicarbonate of soda and salt in a mixing bowl and mix together.

2 Whisk together the eggs and oil then stir into the dry ingredients. Stir in the yoghurt then gradually stir in the milk until the mixture is a smooth batter.

3 Stir in the chopped pecans.

4 Grate the zest from 2 of the oranges and stir into the batter. Leave the batter to rest for 10 minutes. Divide the oranges into segments and keep to one side.

5 Preheat the waffle iron and cook the batter in batches, keeping the cooked waffles warm.

6 Serve the waffles topped with orange segments, a dollop of natural yoghurt and a sprinkling of caster sugar.

Gingerbread waffles

A spicy waffle mixture that is great topped with fruit and maple syrup, or even just a knob of butter. Or top it with peaches and cream, following the recipe on page 92.

Makes 20

- 50 g (2 oz) soft light brown sugar
- 600 g (1 lb 5 oz) plain flour
- 2 tsp baking powder
- 1 tsp bicarbonate of soda
- 1 tsp ground cinnamon
- 1 tsp ground ginger
- 1 tsp ground cloves
- 1 tsp salt
- 700 ml (1¼ pt) skimmed milk
- 175 ml (6 fl oz) vegetable oil
- 4 large eggs, lightly beaten
- Sliced apples and maple syrup to serve

1 Crumble the brown sugar to remove all lumps and place in a mixing bowl with the flour, baking powder, bicarbonate of soda and spices and mix well.

2 Add the milk, oil and eggs and stir until blended and smooth. Leave to stand for 10 minutes.

3 Preheat a waffle iron. Cook the waffles in batches, keeping the cooked ones warm.

4 Serve topped with apple slices and pour over maple syrup.

Caramelised apple pancakes

Caramelising fruit with a little sugar makes them deliciously syrupy. These pancakes are great served with crème fraiche.

erves 4

- 40 g (1 ½ oz) unsalted butter
- 2 tbsp caster sugar
- 3 medium eating apples, peeled, cored and cut into thin wedges
- 100 g (4 oz) plain flour
- 2 medium eggs
- 1 tsp muscovado sugar
- Pinch ground cinnamon
- 200 ml (7 fl oz) milk
- 75 ml (3 fl oz) water
- 1 tsp vegetable oil

1 Melt the butter in a frying pan. Sprinkle over the sugar then stir until dissolved.

2 Add the apple slices and cook for 5–10 minutes, turning gently, until soft and just golden. Keep warm.

3 For the pancakes, put the flour in a bowl and make a well in the centre. Break the eggs into the well and whisk, bringing in the flour from the edges. Add the sugar and cinnamon. Mix together the milk and water and gradually whisk into the egg batter.

4 Heat a non-stick frying pan and wipe with a tiny amount of oil. Pour a ladle of batter into the pan and swirl around to cover the base. Cook for 4 minutes then cook the other side for 2 minutes. Repeat with the remaining batter.

5 Divide the apples between the pancakes, fold over and serve.

FRUIT

Mexican bananas

An unusual way to serve tortillas – crisp on the outside but
filled with soft cooked banana and spicy muscovado syrup,
topped with orange flavoured Greek yoghurt.

Serves 4

- 4 flour tortillas
- 4 bananas, peeled and
  cut lengthways
- 8 tsp muscovado sugar
- 1 tsp ground cinnamon
- Grated rind of 1 orange
- 200 g (7 oz) Greek yoghurt

1 Preheat the oven to 180°C
(350°F/Gas Mark 4).

2 Place a tortilla on the work surface and
put a banana in the middle of it.

3 Sprinkle with 2 tsp muscovado sugar and
the cinnamon then wrap the tortilla
around the filling and secure with a
cocktail stick.

4 Bake in the oven for 8–10 minutes until
the muscodavo sugar has turned to syrup
and the tortilla is crisp.

5 Stir the grated orange rind into the
yoghurt and serve each tortilla with a big
dollop of this on top, remembering to
remove the cocktail stick first!

Yoghurt raspberry fool

Making fruit fools is so easy and far tastier than the ones you can buy – substitute your favourite fruits for variety. This is the healthy version, using yoghurt and fromage frais, you could substitute either of these with whipped double cream to make it even naughtier!

Serves 4

- 100 g (3½ oz) natural yoghurt
- 50 g (1¾ oz) fromage frais
- 300 g (10½ oz) fresh raspberries, slightly crushed
- 1 tbsp honey
- Few sprigs fresh mint

1 Mix together the yoghurt and fromage frais then gently stir in the raspberries.

2 Spoon into 4 bowls and drizzle with the honey. Garnish each one with a sprig of mint.

Exotic fruit salad

We are now lucky enough to get exotic fruits nearly all the year round, so make the most of them and bring a little sunshine into your morning!

Serves 6

- 12 lychees, peeled and stoned
- 1 small pineapple, peeled, cored and cut into bite-size pieces
- 2 mangoes, peeled, stoned and cut into bite-size pieces
- 1 pomegranate, seeds removed
- 6 Medjool dates, stoned, and diced
- 5 passion fruit
- Crème fraîche and ground nutmeg to serve

1 Place the lychees, pineapple chunks, mango pieces, pomegranate seeds and diced dates in a large bowl.

2 Scrape the seeds from the passion fruits and gently stir through the salad. Serve immediately with dollops of crème fraîche sprinkled with ground nutmeg.

Forest fruit croissant

For a really warming autumn brunch, try warm fruits and a drop of cassis, a thick blackcurrant liqueur, on a crisp buttery hot croissant.

Serves 4

- 125 g (4½ oz) blackberries
- 2 eating apples, peeled and sliced
- Grated rind and juice of 1 orange
- 2 tbsp sugar
- 4 butter croissants
- 4 tbsp crème fraîche
- 2 tbsp cassis

1 Put the blackberries, apples, orange rind and juice and sugar in a small pan and simmer for 12–15 minutes until the apples are starting to soften.

2 Slice the croissants in half horizontally then warm them in a warm oven or under the grill just to crisp them slightly.

3 Place the bottom half of each croissant on a plate and top with the fruit compote.

4 Add a dollop of crème fraîche then drizzle this with cassis. Place the top back on at an angle and serve immediately.

Plum and mango tart

If you are scared of making the pastry you can substitute ready-made – nobody will know! Most fruits work well in a tart, try peaches and raspberries or pears and blackberries.

Serves 4–6

- 175 g (6 oz) plain flour
- 75 g (2¾ oz) butter, chilled and cut into small cubes
- 5 plums, stoned and quartered
- 2–3 mangoes, stoned, peeled and cut into slices
- 2 tbsp caster sugar
- 1 tbsp cornflour
- Crème fraîche or natural yoghurt to serve

1 Preheat the oven to 200°C (400°F/Gas Mark 6).

2 Sift the flour into a mixing bowl, add the butter and rub in with your fingertips.

3 Sprinkle with 2 tbsp cold water and stir to moisten and gradually bring the pastry together. Knead briefly on a floured work surface then chill for 20 minutes.

4 Place the fruit in a bowl then stir in the sugar and cornflour.

5 Roll the pastry large enough to line a 22-cm (9-in) tart tin, with 2 cm (¾ in) spare around the edge. Spoon the fruit evenly into the pastry case then fold over the edges of the pastry, leaving the centre uncovered.

6 Bake for 30–35 minutes until the pastry is golden and the fruits are soft. Serve warm with dollops of crème fraîche or natural yoghurt.

Spicy baked pears

These are perfect to serve for a winter brunch – quite light but really delicious and pears are at their best at this time of year.

Serves 6

- 25 g (1 oz) butter, softened
- 50 g (1¾ oz) soft light brown sugar
- 1 egg yolk
- 100 g (3½ oz) almond macaroons, crumbled
- 6 ripe pears
- 2–3 tbsp Grand Marnier
- 200 g (7 oz) Greek yoghurt
- Sprinkling of ground cinnamon

1 Preheat the oven to 180°C (350°F/Gas Mark 4).

2 Cream together the butter and sugar in a bowl. Stir in the egg yolk and the crumbled macaroons.

3 Cut the pears in half and cut out the stalk, leaving a little dip in the centre of each half. Place on a buttered baking tray.

4 Divide the macaroon mixture between the pear halves, pressing it down quite well.

5 Sprinkle over the Grand Marnier and bake for about 25 minutes, until soft.

6 Serve with a dollop of Greek yoghurt and a sprinkling of ground cinnamon on each one.

Malt loaf with grilled figs and crème fraîche

If you can't get malt loaf then any fruit bread would be just as good – or try using fruit cake, or maybe left over Christmas cake for a really indulgent Boxing Day brunch!

Serves 4

- 8 slices malt loaf
- 8 tsp crème fraîche
- 4 figs, halved
- 4 tsp honey
- $1/4$ tsp grated nutmeg

1 Heat a griddle pan until very hot.

2 Spread each slice of malt loaf with 1 tsp crème fraîche.

3 Place the figs on the griddle, cut side down and cook for 3–4 minutes until starting to caramelize.

4 Divide the malt loaf slices between 4 plates and top with the grilled figs.

5 Pour over the honey and sprinkle with grated nutmeg. Serve immediately.

Orchard fruit and berry sponge

This is so delicious and could even be served for afternoon tea – if there is any left! Eat it as it is or with a big dollop of natural yoghurt or crème fraîche.

Makes 8 slices

- 750 g (1 lb 10 oz) apple and pears, peeled, cored and chopped
- 4 tbsp honey
- 1 tsp mixed spice
- 120 g (3³/₄ oz) butter
- 120 g (3³/₄ oz) light soft brown sugar
- 2 medium eggs, beaten
- 285 g (10 oz) self raising flour, sieved
- 150 g (5¹/₂ oz) blackberries
- 1 eating apple, cored and finely sliced

1 Preheat the oven to 180°C (350°F/Gas Mark 4). Butter and base line a 20-cm (8-in) round loosed-bottomed cake tin.

2 Gently simmer the apples and pears with a little water for 10–12 minutes, until just soft. Add 3 tbsp of the honey and the mixed spice and heat through for 1–2 minutes then leave to cool.

3 Cream together the butter and sugar until pale and fluffy then gradually beat in the eggs. Fold in the flour then stir in the apples and pears and half the blackberries.

4 Spoon the mixture into the prepared tin. Decorate the top with the thinly sliced apple and remaining blackberries.

5 Bake for 45–50 minutes, until golden and cooked through – test by sticking a knife in the centre, the knife should come out clean.

Drizzle with the remaining honey and leave to cool for a few minutes in the tin before turning out and cooling completely on a wire cooling rack. Dust with sifted icing sugar to serve.

Plum and rhubarb compote

Rhubarb was originally grown in Britain in the fourteenth century as a medicinal herb. Luckily somebody realised how delicious it is so now we can all appreciate it! To get the best flavour try and eat it only when it is in season.

Serves 4

- 450 g (1 lb) rhubarb, cut into 6-cm (2½-in) slices
- 8 plums, stoned and halved
- 3–4 tbsp dark muscovado sugar

1 Preheat the oven to 150°C (300°F/Gas Mark 2).

2 Place the rhubarb, plums and sugar in an ovenproof dish and sprinkle with the sugar.

3 Cover loosely with foil and bake for 20 minutes. Check the rhubarb is cooked through then leave to cool slightly before serving with natural yoghurt or crème fraîche. This can also be eaten cold.

Baked honey figs

**A fantastic way to enjoy figs when they are at their best –
this recipe would also impress guests if served for lunch,
with a beautiful vanilla ice-cream.**

Serves 4

- Juice of 1 orange
- 2 tbsp honey
- 16 figs
- 16 walnut halves or whole blanched almonds
- 16 small pieces orange peel

1 Put the orange juice in a pan and add 2 tbsp water. Add the honey and bring to the boil.

2 Add the figs and cook gently for about 15 minutes. Drain and reserve the liquid. Leave the figs to cool.

3 Preheat the oven to 200°C (400°F/Gas Mark 6).

4 Make a slit in each fig and place a walnut halve and piece of orange peel in each.

5 Place the stuffed figs on a baking tray and bake for 15–20 minutes, until caramelised.

6 Serve drizzled with the honey syrup.

MEAT

AND

FISH

Steak and egg sandwich

A steak sandwich can be served at any time of day – the addition of a fried egg makes it more breakfast-like. Add some of your favourite relish to really spice it up.

Serves 1

- 1 ciabatta roll
- 1 tsp wholegrain mustard
- 1 minute steak
- 1 tsp olive oil
- 1 egg
- 1/4 red onion, sliced thinly
- 25 g (1 oz) rocket leaves
- Freshly ground black pepper

1 Slice the ciabatta roll in half horizontally. Spread each half with the wholegrain mustard.

2 Heat a griddle and cook the steak for a minute on either side (depending on how rare you like your steak).

3 Meanwhile heat the oil in a frying pan and fry the egg.

4 Place the red onion and rocket on the base of the ciabatta roll then top with the steak and finally the egg. Sprinkle with black pepper and serve immediately.

Club sandwich

A 'serious' sandwich that will certainly keep hunger at bay for quite a while. If you don't have bacon, ham can be used instead. Traditionally served with a handful of potato crisps.

Serves 2

- 6 rashers streaky bacon
- 6 slices white bread
- 4 tbsp mayonnaise
- 2 tsp Dijon mustard
- 3 tomatoes, thinly sliced
- 125 g (4½ oz) cooked chicken, shredded
- Handful of mixed salad leaves

1 Grill the rashers of bacon until crisp.

2 Toast the bread on both sides. Spread 4 slices with mayonnaise and 2 with mustard.

3 Place two pieces of toast spread with mayonnaise on a breadboard and top with the grilled bacon and sliced tomatoes.

4 Place the toast spread with mustard on top of the sliced tomatoes.

5 Top each of these slices with shredded chicken and salad leaves then finish with the remaining toast.

6 Place 4 cocktail sticks in each quarter of the sandwich before cutting into quarters.

Bacon, potato and onion sauté

A real comfort or hangover food for those days when you need serious brunch – serve this with eggs, either poached or fried, or with really good thick grilled sausages.

Serves 4–6

- 700 g (1 lb 9 oz) potatoes, peeled and diced
- 1 tbsp olive oil
- 6 rashers back bacon, diced
- 2 onions, peeled and sliced
- 150 ml (5 fl oz) double cream
- 2 eggs
- Salt and freshly ground black pepper
- 100 g (3½ oz) cheddar cheese, grated

1 Preheat the oven to 200°C (400°F/Gas Mark 6).

2 Put the potatoes in a pan and cover with water. Bring to the boil then simmer for 2 minutes. Drain.

3 Heat the oil in a frying pan and fry the bacon for 4–5 minutes. Remove with a slotted spoon and then add the onion to the pan. Sauté for 3–4 minutes.

4 Mix together the cream and eggs in a large bowl and add the seasoning and half the grated cheese.

5 Mix in the potatoes, onion and bacon then pour this mixture into a buttered ovenproof dish.

6 Top with the remaining cheese and bake for 35–40 minutes until golden. Serve immediately, either on its own or with grilled sausages.

Chicken and pepper omelette

Omelettes are the perfect brunch for one, and pretty much anything goes well in them. Check out what's in your fridge and then make an omelette to eat it in! Tomatoes, ham, cheese, prawns, asparagus – the list is endless.

Serves 1

- 1 tbsp olive oil
- $1/4$ red pepper, deseeded and thinly sliced
- $1/4$ green pepper, deseeded and thinly sliced
- 3 eggs, beaten
- Salt and freshly ground black pepper
- 100 g ($3^1/_2$ oz) cooked chicken, shredded
- 40 g ($1^1/_2$ oz) cheddar cheese, grated

1 Heat the oil in an omelette pan and cook the sliced peppers for 2–3 minutes until starting to soften. Remove from the pan with a slotted spoon.

2 Preheat the grill. Season the beaten eggs then pour in the hot pan. Move around with a spatula as they start to cook to let the uncooked egg reach the pan.

3 When the egg starts to set add the shredded chicken and peppers, sprinkling them evenly over the omelette.

4 When the omelette is set underneath and the top is still a little soft, sprinkle over the cheese and place under a hot grill. Cook until bubbling and golden and serve immediately with a crisp green salad.

Chorizo stuffed tortilla

Chorizo are long thin Spanish sausages whose characteristic flavouring is paprika – some are hotter than others! Served with a spicy tomato salsa this is a vibrant brunch dish.

Serves 4

- 4 tortillas, warmed
- 4 tbsp tomato salsa
- 75 g (3 oz) chorizo, thinly sliced
- ¼ cucumber, cut into julienne strips
- 1 red pepper, deseeded and cut into julienne strips
- 2 tbsp shredded iceburg lettuce
- few sprigs of coriander

1 Place the tortillas on a chopping board and spread each one with a tbsp of tomato salsa.

2 Divide the chorizo between the tortillas and then top with the cucumber, red pepper, iceburg lettuce and coriander.

3 Roll up tightly then slice diagonally across the middle. Wrap in a napkin to serve.

English muffins with spicy sausage

This is like having a full English breakfast, minus the egg, on a muffin! If you really want to go mad why not fry and egg and place it on top too! Use really good pork sausages from your butcher.

Serves 4

- 1 tbsp olive oil
- 4 pork sausages
- 4 rashers streaky bacon, chopped
- 1 small onion, peeled and thinly sliced
- 1/2 tsp chilli flakes (according to taste)
- 50 g (2 oz) mushrooms, sliced
- 12 cherry tomatoes, halved
- 4 English muffins, sliced ~ in half horizontally

1 Heat the oil in a frying pan and add the sausages. Cook for 4–5 minutes, turning occasionally.

2 Add the chopped bacon and onion and continue to cook for another 5–6 minutes.

3 Stir in the chilli flakes and mushrooms and cook for a further 3–4 minutes.

4 Take out each sausage, one at a time, and slice into 4 pieces then return to the pan.

5 Finally, add the cherry tomatoes and cook for 2–3 minutes more.

6 Toast the muffins and place two halves on each plate. Top with the spicy sausage mixture and serve immediately.

Croque Monsieur

This French classic is delicious served on its own or with French mustard. A Croque Madame is with the addition of a poached egg on top!

Serves 2

- 2 eggs
- 1 tbsp double cream
- Salt and freshly ground black pepper
- 4 slices ham
- 4 slices thick white bread
- 100 g (3½ oz) Gruyère cheese, grated
- 40 g (1½ oz) butter

1 Beat the eggs, cream and seasoning together in a large bowl.

2 Divide the slices of ham between 2 slices of bread and sprinkle both slices with the grated cheese then top with the remaining slices of bread.

3 Dip each sandwich into the egg mixture, making sure they are well coated.

4 Heat the butter in a frying pan and cook the Croque Monsieur on both sides until golden. Serve warm.

Brunch paella

Paella is traditionally served in Spain with chicken and lots of fresh seafood, and normally in a large paella pan big enough to serve a whole party! This version has slightly less seafood but is delicious served for brunch.

Serves 4

- 50 g (1¾ oz) butter
- 1 tbsp olive oil
- 6 rashers smoked bacon, chopped
- 1 large onion, peeled and chopped
- 2 cloves garlic, crushed
- 225 g (8 oz) long grain rice
- 1 litre (1¾ pts) good chicken stock
- 450 g (1 lb) chicken, cut into bite-size pieces
- Pinch of saffron
- 225 g (8 oz) king prawns
- 225 g (8 oz) shell-on mussels
- 6 plum tomatoes, peeled, deseeded and chopped
- Freshly chopped parsley, to garnish

1 Melt the butter in a large frying pan with the olive oil, cook the bacon for 4–5 minutes then remove with a slotted spoon and keep to one side.

2 Add the onion and garlic and cook for 1–2 minutes, until softened, before adding the rice – stir and cook for 1–2 minutes to coat with the onion and garlic.

3 Pour the stock in to the pan, stirring, and then add the chicken. Cover the pan and cook very gently for 15–20 minutes, or until the rice is nearly cooked.

4 Stir in the saffron, prawns and mussels and cook for 2–3 minutes until the mussel shells open (discard any that don't).

5 Stir in the tomatoes, season and serve immediately.

Spicy sausage patties

Treat yourself to some special sausages to use in this recipe – pork and leek are great with these spices – add more if you want a really spicy start to the day!

Serves 4

- 8 good pork sausages
- 1 apple, peeled, cored and grated
- 2 cloves garlic, crushed
- 1 tsp cumin seeds
- 1/2 tsp ground coriander
- 1/2 tsp chilli flakes
- 1 tbsp freshly chopped parsley
- 1 tbsp olive oil

1 Cut the skins off the sausages and place the sausage meat into a large bowl.

2 Add the grated apple, crushed garlic, spices and chopped parsley.

3 Using your hands, mix together well and then form onto 8 little patty shapes. Chill for 30 minutes.

4 Heat the oil in a frying pan and fry the patties well on both sides to ensure they are cooked through.

5 Serve with scrambled eggs and grilled tomatoes.

Sausage and egg pitta pockets

These are great to serve to children – little pockets of bread stuffed with egg and sausages. A little tomato ketchup may also be a good idea.

Serves 4

- 8 good-quality sausages
- 4 eggs
- 4 pitta breads – white or wholemeal
- 4 tbsp mayonnaise
- Handful of rocket

1 Grill or fry the sausages until they are golden and cooked through.

2 Hard boil the eggs for 8 minutes then refresh under cold water to prevent greying around the edge of the yolk. When they are cool enough to handle peel off the shells. Slice the boiled eggs.

3 Toast the pitta breads on both sides then cut in half horizontally.

4 Chop the sausages into big chunks.

5 Spoon a little mayonnaise into each pocket and then stuff with the sausage, egg and rocket. Serve whilst still warm.

Chicken and blue cheese melt

This is actually an open sandwich that you will need a knife and fork for – the blue cheese will ooze everywhere, just as it should! A great way to use any left over chicken from a roast meal.

Serves 2

- 2 thick slices wholemeal bread
- 1 tbsp mango chutney
- 150 g (5½ oz) cooked chicken, shredded or chopped
- 2 spring onions, thinly sliced
- 100 g (3½ oz) blue cheese

1 Heat the grill and toast the slices of bread on both sides.

2 Spread both slices with the mango chutney then top with the chicken and spring onion.

3 Crumble over the blue cheese and place under the grill again. Cook for 2–3 minutes or until the cheese is bubbling and starting to turn golden.

Cod and haddock fishcakes

These delicious fishcakes can be made with different types of fish (cod, salmon, haddock trout) and herbs (dill, parsley, thyme), just choose your favourite. You can also make the mixture in advance and keep it chilled until you are ready to cook them.

Serves 4

- 250 g (9 oz) cod, cooked and flaked
- 200 g (7 oz) haddock, cooked and flaked
- 350 g (12 oz) mashed potatoes
- Salt and freshly ground black pepper
- 25 g (1 oz) butter, melted
- 1 tbsp freshly chopped chives
- 2 eggs, beaten
- 3 tbsp white breadcrumbs
- 4 tbsp sunflower oil for frying

1 Mix together the fish, potatoes and seasoning. Add the melted butter, chopped chives and enough egg to bind together – not too wet. Leave to cool in the fridge for 30 minutes.

2 Using wet hands, shape the mixture into 8 flat cakes. Dip the cakes in the remaining beaten egg and then into the breadcrumbs to coat.

3 Heat half the oil in a frying pan and cook 4 fishcakes for about 4–5 minutes on either side, until golden. Repeat with the remaining oil and fishcakes and serve immediately with lemon wedges and a crisp green salad.

Danish open sandwich

Not only is herring extremely tasty, it is good for you too – lots of omega oils. Cured herrings can be bought in a variety of sauces and marinades – dill, sherry etc. Any of these would be perfect in this recipe.

Serves 4

- 2 large cooked beetroot, sliced
- 4 large slices rye or pumpernickel bread
- 300 g (10½ oz) Danish cured herrings
- 8 gherkins, sliced
- 8 sprigs of fresh dill

1 Arrange the slices of beetroot on the slices of bread.

2 Top each slice with the Danish herrings.

3 Garnish with sliced gherkins and dill and serve immediately.

Smoked salmon paté

A quick way to make a nutritious great tasting paté that can be served either with toast or with crudités and a salad. You can also make this with tinned tuna.

Serves 6

- 1 x 213 g (7½ oz) can red salmon, drained
- 100 g (3½ oz) smoked salmon pieces
- 175 g (6 oz) cottage cheese
- Juice of ½ lemon
- Freshly ground black pepper
- Wholemeal bread to serve

1 Flake the tinned salmon into a food processor.

2 Add the smoked salmon pieces, the cottage cheese, lemon juice and pepper and blend until smooth. Transfer to a serving bowl.

3 Serve with toasted wholemeal bread.

Seared tuna with stir-fry vegetables

A very healthy way to start the day – use a variety of vegetables that you like, cutting them into small pieces to cut down on cooking time.

Serves 4

- 2 tbsp vegetable oil
- 3 tbsp cashew nuts
- 1 bunch spring onions, trimmed and sliced
- 3 cm (1½ in) piece fresh ginger, peeled and grated
- 200 g (7 oz) baby sweetcorn, blanched
- 200 g (7 oz) small carrots, peeled and cut into matchstick strips
- 200 g (7 oz) mangetout, shredded
- 200 g (7 oz) beansprouts
- 1 tbsp soy sauce
- 4 tuna steaks
- 2 tbsp sesame seeds, toasted

1 Heat 1 tbsp of the oil in a wok and stir-fry the cashew nuts until starting to brown. Remove from the pan with a slotted spoon.

2 Add the sliced spring onions and grated ginger and stir-fry for 30 seconds before adding the sweetcorn and carrot matchsticks. Stir-fry for 3–4 minutes. Add the mangetout and beansprouts and stir-fry for a further 2 minutes.

3 Heat the remaining oil in a frying pan and when very hot add the tuna. Cook for only 3–4 minutes on either side to sear – leave the middle slightly pink. Turn off the heat and leave in the pan while you finish the stir-fry.

4 Return the cashew nuts to the pan, sprinkle with soy sauce and serve – divide between 4 plates or bowls and top with the seared tuna sprinkled with toasted sesame seeds.

Smoked salmon and egg bagels

Bagels are characteristic of Jewish and particularly New York Jewish cuisine. They are traditionally served with salt beef or cream cheese and smoked salmon.

Serves 2

- 125 g (4½ oz) smoked salmon, cut into thin strips
- 4 tbsp single cream
- 2 bagels, halved
- 15 g (½ oz) butter
- 4 eggs
- Salt and freshly ground black pepper

1 Place the smoked salmon strips in a bowl and pour in the cream.

2 Lightly toast the bagel halves on both sides.

3 Melt the butter in a pan. Break the eggs into a bowl and whisk lightly with a fork.

4 When the butter is foaming pour the eggs in and stir continuously until they start to solidify. Quickly pour in the salmon and cream and continue to cook and stir until the liquid has gone.

5 Check for seasoning then spoon over the toasted bagels and serve immediately.

Smoked haddock with cream and chives

Quite an indulgent way to serve a healthy fish – but great for a treat! Serve with crusty wholemeal toast to mop up the juices.

Serves 4

- 225 g (8 oz) smoked haddock, cooked and flaked
- 3 tbsp single cream
- Juice of ½ lemon
- 3 spring onions, finely chopped
- 50 g (1¾ oz) butter
- 6 eggs
- Salt and freshly ground black pepper
- 1 tbsp freshly chopped chives
- Wholemeal toast, to serve

1 Mix together the flaked haddock, cream, lemon juice and spring onion and leave to one side.

2 Heat the butter in a large non-stick frying pan.

3 When the butter is melted and foaming add the eggs and gently break the yolks. Continue pushing the egg mixture in towards the middle from the outside of the pan to enable any uncooked egg to reach the pan.

4 When the eggs are beginning to set, add the haddock mixture and stir until the eggs are just cooked to the consistency you like.

5 Season and scatter with chives and serve immediately with wholemeal toast.

Crab and egg New Orleans style

Fresh crabmeat is delicious served with a creamy white sauce, and the addition of a softly poached egg make this recipe a delight to eat. If you can't get fresh crabmeat frozen will do.

Serves 6

- 100 g (3½ oz) butter
- 3 tbsp plain flour
- 300 ml (½ pt) milk
- Salt and freshly ground black pepper
- Dash of Tabasco
- 450 g (1 lb) fresh crabmeat
- 6 eggs
- 3 English muffins
- Few pinches of paprika

1 Melt 50 g (1¾ oz) of the butter in a small pan and then stir in the flour, making a roux. Gradually add the milk, whisking continuously and then bring to a simmer. The sauce should be thick and creamy. Stir in the seasoning and Tabasco to your liking.

2 Melt the remaining butter and gently stir the crabmeat into this.

3 Softly poach the eggs in a pan of boiling water.

4 Toast the muffins and place one half on each plate. Divide the buttery crabmeat between the muffin halves then place a poached egg on top of each one.

5 Pour over the sauce and sprinkle with paprika before serving.

VEGETARIAN

Boston baked beans

A great way to spice up a tin of beans and make them go further – use stronger curry powder if you dare! Serve on wholemeal toast or with fried sausages and eggs.

Serves 2

- 1 tbsp olive oil
- 1 large onion, peeled and chopped
- ½ tsp medium curry powder
- 40 g (1½ oz) raisins
- 1 × 415 g (14 oz) can baked beans
- 3 tbsp mango chutney
- 25 g (1 oz) flaked almonds

1 Heat the oil in a pan and sauté the onion for 4–5 minutes, until softening.

2 Stir in the curry powder and cook for about 2 minutes before adding the raisins, baked beans and mango chutney.

3 Cook for 4–5 minutes, stirring occasionally to enable everything to heat through.

4 Serve on crusty wholemeal toast sprinkled with the flaked almonds.

Brunch enchiladas

Flour tortillas are so versatile, you can vary the fillings to suit – prawns, ham, or cold chicken would also be good. Just always make sure there is lots of melting cheese.

Serves 4

- 2 tbsp olive oil
- 1 onion, peeled and chopped
- 2 cloves garlic, crushed
- 1 tsp ground cumin
- 1 tsp dried oregano
- 2 × 400 g (14 oz) tins chopped tomatoes
- 1 tsp caster sugar
- 1 tbsp tomato purée
- Salt and freshly ground black pepper
- 8 flour tortillas
- 16 cherry tomatoes, halved
- 1 bunch spring onions, trimmed and sliced
- 250 g (9 oz) cheddar cheese, grated
- Sour cream and diced avocado to serve

1 Preheat the oven to 180°C (350°F/Gas Mark 4).

2 Heat the oil in a pan and sauté the onion for 2–3 minutes until softening. Add the garlic, cumin and oregano and stir.

3 Add the tinned tomatoes, sugar and purée, bring to a simmer and cook for 15–20 minutes. Season to taste.

4 Taking one tortilla at a time, spread a spoonful of the tomato sauce over the tortilla, sprinkle with halved cherry tomatoes, chopped spring onions and grated cheese. Roll tightly and place in an ovenproof dish. Repeat with the remaining tortillas.

5 Spoon over any remaining sauce and sprinkle with remaining grated cheese. Bake for 20–25 minutes.

6 Serve hot with a dish of soured cream and some diced avocado.

Mushroom crostini

Crostini comes from the Italian word 'crosta' – crust. These little toasted slices of bread are great with lots of toppings – pâté, roasted peppers, parma ham, tomato and basil.

Serves 4

- 4 tbsp olive oil
- 1 fat clove garlic, peeled and crushed
- 1 small thin French stick, cut into 12 slices
- 250 g (9 oz) chestnut mushrooms, chopped
- 2 tbsp freshly chopped parsley
- Salt and freshly ground black pepper
- 40 g (1½ oz) Parmesan, shaved

1 Preheat the oven to 200°C (400°F/Gas Mark 6).

2 Drizzle 3 tbsp of the olive oil on a baking tray, add the garlic and then, using your hands, spread the oil and garlic all over the tray. Add the slices of bread, rubbing and turning them until they are coated with the garlicky oil.

3 Bake for 10–15 minutes until golden. Keep an eye on them to prevent them from becoming too brown.

4 Heat the remaining oil in a frying pan and cook the mushrooms for 8–10 minutes.

5 Stir in the parsley and seasoning then top each slice of bread with the mushroom mixture.

6 Sprinkle with shaved parmesan and serve immediately before the bread starts to go soft.

Devilled tomatoes

Polenta is like a thick porridge made from maize and is the staple carbohydrate dish of northern Italy. It is a little like pasta in that it takes on the flavours of whatever you add to it – in this case the spicy juices from the tomatoes.

Serves 4

- 4 large slices of ready-to-use polenta
- 3 tbsp olive oil
- 100 g (3^1/$_2$ oz) cheddar cheese, grated
- 12 tomatoes, sliced horizontally
- 2 cloves garlic, peeled and crushed
- 1 tsp dry mustard powder
- ^{1}/$_2$ tsp ground cumin
- ^{1}/$_2$ tsp curry powder
- 4 tbsp mango chutney

1 Brush the polenta slices with a little olive oil and grill for 5 minutes on one side. Turn over, sprinkle with cheese and grill for another 3–5 minutes.

2 Place the tomato halves on a large piece of foil, cut side down and place under a hot grill for 3–4 minutes.

3 Turn the tomatoes over. Mix the remaining oil with the garlic, mustard powder and spices and spoon a little over each tomato. Grill for another 3–4 minutes.

4 Spread each slice of polenta with a little mango chutney and top with the curried tomatoes.

Sweetcorn fritters

Perfect for a summers day, served with a fresh herb and tomato salsa. If you can't get fresh corn on the cob use either frozen or tinned sweetcorn instead.

rves 4

4 corn on the cob
4 tbsp double cream
2 tbsp plain flour, sifted
$1/2$ tsp baking powder
$1/2$ tsp sugar
Salt and freshly ground black pepper
1 tbsp olive oil
Salsa of your choice to serve

1 Cook the corn in boiling water for 5–6 minutes, until tender. Drain.

2 Cut the kernels off the corn with a sharp knife – hold the corn on its end and run the knife downwards – keep turning until all the kernels are have been cut off.

3 Put the kernels and any juices in a bowl with the cream, flour, baking powder, sugar, salt and pepper and mix well.

4 Heat the olive oil in a frying pan and drop tablespoons of the corn batter into the pan, flattening them slightly. Cook for 4–5 minutes on either side, until golden.

5 Drain on kitchen paper and keep warm while you cook the remaining batter.

6 Serve with salsa.

Hash browns

A real American way with potatoes – the original name which was recorded in 1900 was 'Hashed Brown Potatoes' – basically it is grated potatoes, with a few other ingredients, formed into little cakes then fried. These are great to serve with a fried egg.

Serves 4

- 6 medium potatoes, peeled
- 1 small onion, peeled
- 1 large egg, beaten
- 1 tbsp plain flour
- 2 tbsp freshly chopped herbs
  (parsley, chives,
  rosemary, thyme)
- 1 tbsp olive oil
- Salt and freshly ground
  black pepper
- 2 tbsp vegetable oil

1 Coarsely grate the potatoes and onion into a clean cloth. Squeeze out any excess liquid then transfer the grated potato and onion to a bowl.

2 Add the beaten egg, flour, chopped herbs, olive oil and seasoning and mix well.

3 Heat 1 tsp of vegetable oil in a frying pan and add tablespoon of the potato mixture. Press down flat gently with a spatula or fish slice to make a pattie shape and cook both sides for 4–5 minutes until golden.

4 Keep them warm while you repeat with the remaining oil and mixture.

5 Serve with grilled tomatoes and fried eggs.

Herbed potato pie

A great way to serve potatoes – layers of potatoes, cheese and herbs cooked in stock until meltingly delicious. Use your favourite herb or a selection of different ones.

Serves 4

- 5 large baking potatoes, peeled
- 2 cloves garlic, peeled and crushed
- 3 shallots, peeled and sliced
- 2 tbsp freshly chopped herbs (parsley, chives, rosemary, thyme)
- 125 g (4$\frac{1}{2}$ oz) cheddar cheese, grated
- 50 g (1$\frac{3}{4}$ oz) Parmesan, grated
- 425 ml (15 fl oz) vegetable stock

1 Preheat the oven to 180°C (350°F/Gas Mark 4).

2 Slice the potatoes very thinly. Butter an ovenproof dish and layer one third of the potatoes in the dish.

3 Sprinkle over one third of the garlic, shallots, herbs and grated cheese.

4 Repeat the layers two more times until all the ingredients are used.

5 Sprinkle the top with grated Parmesan and pour over the hot stock.

6 Bake in the oven for 30–40 minutes or until the potatoes are soft and the cheese is golden.

Mexican fried potatoes

In Mexico you would probably have these with some refried beans but if you can't find those try serving them topped with a poached egg or with crisp bacon if wished.

Serves 4

- 3 tbsp olive oil
- 900 g (2 lb) potatoes, peeled and diced
- 1 onion, peeled and diced
- 1 green pepper, deseeded and thinly sliced
- 1 red chilli, deseeded and sliced
- 2 tomatoes, peeled and chopped
- Salt and freshly ground black pepper
- 125 g (4$\frac{1}{2}$ oz) cheese, grated

1 Heat the oil in a large skillet or frying pan and cook the potatoes for 8–10 minutes, stirring occasionally.

2 Add the onion, green pepper and chilli and pat down to a flat layer in the pan. Cook for 5 minutes or until the potatoes are browning underneath.

3 Turn the potatoes over with a spatula and add the chopped tomatoes. Pat down into a flat layer again and cook until the potatoes are golden underneath.

4 Sprinkle with the cheese and flash under a hot grill until the cheese is bubbling and golden.

DRINKS

Bloody Mary

A great way to kick-start the day! This can be made as strong and spicy as you like it – the more Tabasco you add, the hotter it will get. And if you want a non-alcoholic version, known as a Virgin Mary, just leave out the vodka.

Serves 1

- 40 ml (1½ fl oz) vodka
- 100 ml (3½ fl oz) tomato juice
- Squeeze of lemon juice
- 1 tsp Worcestershire sauce
- 3 drops Tabasco (optional)
- Freshly ground black pepper
- Pinch celery salt
- Stick of celery

1 Mix together the vodka, tomato juice, lemon juice, Worcestershire sauce, Tabasco and pepper in jug.

2 Pour into an ice-filled glass.

3 Serve sprinkled with celery salt and a stick of celery for stirring.

Iced coffee

A great way to enjoy a coffee on a hot day. This is more like a coffee milkshake, lovely and creamy, or can be poured over more ice if you want to make it more refreshing.

Serves 1

* 1 tsp instant coffee granules
* 4 tbsp double cream
* 4 ice cubes
* 2 tsp sugar
* 50 ml (2 fl oz) water
* Drop vanilla essence

I Place all the ingredients into a blender or food processor and blend until smooth and frothy. Check sweetness is to your liking and adjust if necessary.
Serve immediately.

Spicy hot chocolate

**A comforting drink for a chilly winter's evening.
Use really good dark chocolate for this, it will make the end
result much tastier. You will never again reach for the
powdered chocolate!**

*rves 2

85 g (3 oz) plain chocolate,
broken into pieces
1 tbsp caster sugar
1 large pinch ground
cinnamon
1 vanilla pod, split lengthways
300 ml ($^1/_2$ pt) milk
100 ml ($3^1/_2$ fl oz) whipping
cream, whipped
Freshly grated chocolate
to serve

1 Warm two big mugs by pouring in boiling water and leaving to stand while you make the hot chocolate.

2 Put the chocolate pieces, sugar, cinnamon, vanilla pod and milk into a small pan and heat gently until the chocolate has melted, stirring occasionally.

3 Bring to the boil and whisk until the chocolate is very smooth and frothy.

4 Remove the vanilla pod.

5 Pour the chocolate into the warmed mugs (having poured out the boiling water) and top with the whipped cream and grated chocolate.

Cantaloupe and raspberry smoothie

A great summer drink that is also healthy and, with cantaloupe melon, is great for your skin! Other fruits can also be used so play around to find your favourites, trying to use those in season for the most flavour.

Serves 2

- 1 cantaloupe melon, deseeded, peeled and cut into chunks
- 150 g (5½ oz) raspberries
- 300 ml (10 fl oz) natural yoghurt
- 100 ml (3½ fl oz) milk
- Ice cubes
- Pinch of ground ginger
- Strawberries to garnish

1 Place all the ingredients into a blender or food processor and blitz until smooth.

2 Pour into ice-filled glasses, sprinkle with pinch of ground ginger and garnish with hulled fresh strawberry slices.

Fresh ginger and lemon tea

If you have the start of a cold then a cup of fresh ginger and lemon tea will help to clear your head – the spiciness of the ginger and the great citrus lemon flavour are perfect for waking up your senses!

Serves 1

- 2.5 cm (1 in) piece of fresh ginger, scrubbed
- 1 stick cinnamon
- Juice of 1 lemon
- ¹/₂ tsp honey (optional)

1 Slice the ginger and place in a mug with the cinnamon stick. Pour over boiling water to fill the cup, and leave to infuse for 1–2 minutes.

2 Strain and stir in the lemon juice, check for sweetness and add honey if required.

Fresh carrot, ginger and apple juice

Ginger is a great spice for your health as it slows down digestion helping your body to take on more nutrients. It is also very strong when used fresh so do taste as you add the juice.

Serves 2

3 large carrots
2 eating apples
2 cm ($^3/_4$ in) piece of fresh ginger, peeled

1 Place the carrots and apples in a juicer and squeeze the juice into two glasses.

2 Juice the fresh ginger and add to the carrot and apple juice to the strength of your liking, mix very well– fresh ginger juice is quite strong so taste as you add!

Summer fruit smoothie

A refreshing summer drink that can also be served poured over ice on a hot day. A perfect way of getting your portions of 5-a-day fruits!

Serves 4

- 1 mango, peeled, deseeded and sliced
- 450 g (1 lb) strawberries, washed and hulled
- 50 g (1³/₄ oz) blueberries
- Grated zest of 1 lemon
- 500 g (1 lb 2 oz) natural yoghurt
- Sprigs of mint to serve

1 Place all the ingredients into a blender or food processor and blitz until smooth.

2 Pour into 2 glasses, either with or without ice.

3 Serve with sprigs of fresh mint.

Muesli smoothie

A great way to have your breakfast on the move – as a drink! Vary the fruits to whatever is in season.

Serves 2

- 2 tbsp muesli
- 2 tbsp natural yoghurt
- 150 ml (5 fl oz) milk
- 100 g (3$^1/_2$ oz) blueberries
- 1 peach, stoned and chopped
- Honey for sweetness, if required

1 Place all the ingredients into a blender or food processor and blend until smooth.

2 Check for sweetness and add honey accordingly.

3 Serve immediately.

Honey nut smoothie

A delicious nutty smoothie, with bananas and honey to add
a touch of sweetness. For extra nutty flavour use soya milk
instead of cow's milk.

Serves 1

- 1 banana, peeled and sliced
- 50 g (1 3/4 oz) hazelnuts
- 300 ml (1/2 pt) semi-skimmed milk (or soya milk)
- 1 tbsp honey
- Pinch of ground cinnamon

1 Place all the ingredients in a blender or food processor and blend until smooth.

2 Pour in a long glass, over ice if wished, and sprinkle a little ground cinnamon on the top to serve.

Homemade lemonade

Just like your grandmother used to make! This bears no relation to the shop bought lemonade you can buy today, this is very zingy and refreshing with a real citrus taste. Serve with more chunks of lemon in the glasses if you wish.

Serves 6

- 3 unwaxed lemons
- 75 g (3 oz) caster sugar (more if wished)
- 1 litre (1³/₄ pts) water, still or sparkling, chilled
- Sprigs of mint to serve

1 Cut the lemons into large chunks and place in a food processor with a third of the sugar and enough water to cover. Process to a mush, then strain.

2 Return the solid bits to the food processor and add another third of sugar and water to cover – process again and then strain.

3 Repeat the process one more time. Taste and adjust the sweetness.

4 Chill for 10 minutes at least.

5 Serve chilled with sprigs of mint, poured into into ice-filled glasses.

Fruit bran milkshake

A great way of getting your daily bran – whizz it up in a blender with you favourite fruit to make a creamy healthy milkshake.

Serves 1

- 100 g (3½ oz) strawberries (or blueberries, raspberries etc)
- 75 g (3 oz) natural yoghurt
- 150 ml (6 fl oz) milk
- 1 tbsp bran
- 1 tsp honey (if required – check sweetness of fruit first)

1 Place all the ingredients into a blender or food processor and blend until smooth.

2 Pour into a long glass and drink immediately.

Tropical refresher

This drink can be quite sharp so feel free to add honey if you need more sweetness – it will depend on the ripeness of the fruit you buy. Always try to buy fruits in season, that way they will have more flavour.

erves 1

125 g (4¹/₂ oz) fresh
pineapple, cored and peeled
1 banana, peeled
2 passion fruit, juice only,
sieve out the pips
200 ml (7 fl oz) natural
yoghurt
200 ml (7 fl oz)
semi-skimmed milk
Shredded coconut to serve

1 Place all the ingredients in a blender or food processor and blend until smooth.

2 Pour into an ice-filled glass and serve sprinkled with shredded coconut.

Index